ユナ、そして こうきしんおうせんな こどもたちへ。
ゆめを みつづけて ください。

For Yoona, and all the other young curious minds.
Never stop dreaming.

みやざき はやお
Hayao Miyazaki

むかしむかし、とうきょうに　みやざきはやお　という
しょうねんが　いました。おとうさんは　ひこうきの
ぶひんを　つくる　かいしゃに　つとめていたので、
はやおは　ひこうきを　みてそだち、ひこうきの
えを　かくのも　だいすきでした。

Once upon a time, in Tokyo, Japan, there was a little boy
named Hayao Miyazaki. His dad worked at a company that
made airplane parts, so Hayao grew up watching airplanes
and loved drawing them, too.

はやおの　おかあさんは　びょうきがちで、にゅういん
せいかつが　ながかったにもかかわらず、あかるく
げんきで、いっしょうけんめい　びょうきと
たたかっていました。

Hayao's mom was often very sick and spent a lot of
time in the hospital. Despite this, she was bright,
lively, and bravely fighting her illness.

このような　けいけんから、はやおは　いろいろな
しょうがいを　のりこえて　せかいを　すくう、
やさしくも　つよいヒロインの　ゆめを
いだくようになりました。

These experiences filled Hayao with dreams of kind
yet strong heroines who could overcome all
obstacles and save the world.

おおきくなるにつれ、はやおは　えいが、
とくに　アニメーションが　だいすきになりました。
あるひ、アニメーションえいがの　なかの　ゆうかんな
しょうじょに　みりょうされた　かれは、じぶんでも
ものがたりを　つくろうと　けついしました。

As he got older, Hayao loved movies, especially animations.
One day, a brave little girl in an animated film captivated him,
and he decided to make his own stories.

だいがくそつぎょうご、はやおは
アニメスタジオで　はたらいていました。
ワクワクする　ものがたりを　たくさん
かんがえ、にほんの　こどもたちを
みりょうしました。

After college, Hayao worked at an animation
studio. He thought up and drew lots of exciting
stories, and kids in Japan loved them.

しかし、はやおのアニメが　すべて　せいこうした　わけ
では　ありませんでした。いっしょうけんめい　えがいた
さくひんが　しっぱいしたときは、がっかりしました。

However, not all of his animations were successful. When
one movie he had worked really hard on became a flop,
Hayao felt sad and disappointed.

しかし、あきらめる　わけにはいかないと　おもい、なにか
ちがうことに　ちょうせんしようと　きめました。

But he knew he couldn't give up. He decided to try something
different—a cartoon series in his own unique style.

このシリーズは、はやおが ずっと えがいていた
とおり、せかいを すくおうとする ゆうかんな
しょうじょ「ナウシカ」を えがいた うつくしい
えいがに なりました。

This series grew into a beautiful movie about a brave girl
named *Nausicaä* who tries to save her world, just as he had
imagined for a long time. Many people loved and praised it.

この　せいこうにより、はやおと　ゆうじんたちは
スタジオジブリを　たちあげ、じぶんたちの　すきなように
もっと　えいがを　つくれる　ように　なりました。

Because of its success, Hayao and his friends started their own place called *Studio Ghibli*, where they could make more movies the way they wanted.

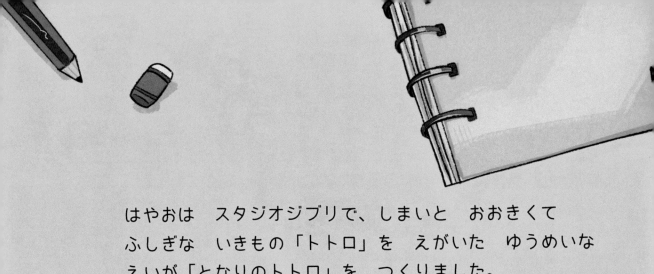

はやおは　スタジオジブリで、しまいと　おおきくて
ふしぎな　いきもの「トトロ」を　えがいた　ゆうめいな
えいが「となりのトトロ」を　つくりました。

At *Studio Ghibli*, Hayao created the famous movie,
My Neighbor Totoro, about two sisters and a giant, friendly
magical creature called Totoro.

この えいがは ゆうじょうと しぜんの
きょういを みごとに えがき、トトロは おとな
から こどもまで あいされる キャラクターに
なりました。

This movie beautifully depicted friendship and the
wonders of nature. To everyone's surprise, Totoro
became a cultural icon, beloved by children and
adults alike.

でも、いいことばかりでは　ありませんでした。ときには、
はやおのアイデアが　ほかの　ひとの　きたい　とは
まったく　ちがう　ことも　ありました。

However, Hayao faced many challenges. Sometimes, his
ideas were quite different from what other people expected.

かれの　さくひんが　すきな　ひとも　いれば、こども
には　むずかしすぎる　という　ひとも　いました。
それでも　はやおは　つくりつづけました。

Some people liked his work, but others thought it was
too complicated or abstract for children.
Regardless, Hayao kept pushing forward.

はやおの　まわりには　ほかの　さいのう　ある　えかき　や
さっかが　いました。はやおたちは　けんめいに　はたらき、
たがいを　ささえあい、たくさんの　ひとを　みりょうする
すばらしい　さくひん　づくりに　うちこみました。

He surrounded himself with other talented artists and
storytellers. They worked hard, supported each other,
and focused on creating even more amazing stories
that touched the hearts of many.

はやおと　ゆうじんたちが　つくる　えいがは
どれも　うつくしい　えいぞう　ばかりでした。

Each film Hayao and his friends made was filled with
adventure and beautiful pictures.

さくひんは　こくさいてきに　ゆうめいな　しょうを
じゅしょうする　ようになり、にほんの　ものがたり
どくとくの　うつくしさが　せかいじゅうの　ファン
に　ひろまりました。

His movies started winning renowned international
awards and introduced global fans to the unique beauty
of Japanese storytelling.

はやおは　せかいじゅうで　ゆうめいに　なりました。
いくさきざきで　かんげいされ、おおくの　ひとが　つぎの
さくひんを　たのしみにしていました。しかし、はやおは
えを　かくのが　だいすきだった　しょうねん　じだいの
ゆめを　ずっと　おぼえていました。

Hayao became famous all over the world. People eagerly welcomed
him everywhere he went, excited to see his next creation. But he
always remembered his dreams as a little
boy who loved to draw.

はやおは　わたしたちに　そうぞうりょくが
おおきな　ゆめに　つながることを　おしえてくれました。
わたしたちに　ひつようなのは、ゆめを　しんじて
どりょくし、けして　あきらめないことです。

Hayao taught us that our imaginations can lead to great
adventures. All we need to do is believe in our dreams,
work hard, and never give up.

Hayao Miyazaki's
Masterpieces

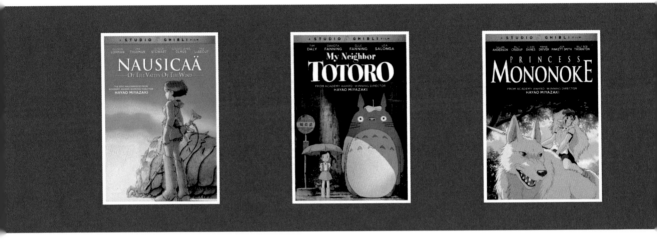

1984
Nausicaä of the Valley
of the Wind

1988
My Neighbor Totoro

1997
Princess Mononoke

In many of Hayao Miyazaki's stories, the main characters are often girls. They are lovely but also bold and brave, ready to solve big problems. Hayao dreamed of a world where strong girls lead the way. Many people loved his idea of girl power, especially since it was unusual at the time.

My Neighbor Totoro was very popular in Japan and loved by animation fans around the world. But it was *Princess Mononoke* that made him famous everywhere.

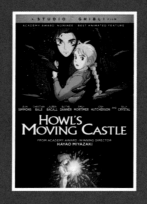

2001

Spirited Away

2004

Howl's Moving Castle

2023

The Boy and
The Heron

After that, *Spirited Away* came out, and people all over the world praised it as a wonderful masterpiece. This made more people discover his earlier movies, making *Studio Ghibli* and Miyazaki famous worldwide.

As he got older, he wanted to share his life stories and ideas with young people. So, at 82, he released his newest movie, *The Boy and The Heron*. This movie won him his first Golden Globe Award. His hard work and dedication made him a master of animation, inspiring many artists around the world.

Photographic acknowledgements (pages 30-31): Amazon.com
All photos of movie posters (pages 30-31) © Studio Ghibli

Other Bilingual Japanese-English Books by the Author

Made in the USA
Las Vegas, NV
20 December 2024

14806282R10021